On the Rise!

by Sue Lennox

Harcourt
SCHOOL PUBLISHERS

Cover, ©Michael Williams/Getty Images; p.3, ©Phil Schermeister/CORBIS; p.6, Library of Congress; p.7, Library of Congress; p.8, ©Jeff Greenberg/The Image Works; p.10, ©Corbis/Punch Stock, p.11, ©Glow Images/Punch Stock; p.12, ©Comstock Images/Punch Stock; p.12, ©Jim Reed/CORBIS; p.13, Austin, Texas from Riverside Park; p.14, Cameraman taking pictures of flood at Portsmouth Ohio.

Printed in China

ISBN 10: 0-15-351033-1
ISBN 13: 978-0-15-351033-5

Ordering Options
ISBN 10: 0-15-350602-4 (Grade 5 On-Level Collection)
ISBN 13: 978-0-15-350602-4 (Grade 5 On-Level Collection)
ISBN 10: 0-5-357958-7 (package of 5)
ISBN 13: 978-0-15-357958-5 (package of 5)

4 5 6 7 8 9 10   0940   12 11 10 09

A gray sky hangs heavy with the promise of rain. Large drops begin to splatter on the ground. Water accumulates in ever-elongating pools on the muddy earth, still soaked from an earlier storm. Puddles feed into small streams that spill into creeks and gullies flowing to the river. Residents of riverfront towns watch anxiously as the water level grows higher and the current grows stronger. Will the river spill its banks? Will people be forced from their homes? These questions have been asked all too often by the many people living on America's floodplains.

What is a floodplain?

A *floodplain* is the area of land next to a river or stream that is likely to become flooded during heavy rains or after snow melts. Modern engineers use something called the 100-year flood rule to figure out the size of a floodplain. They study the history of floods along the waterway as well as changes in the land. They then use this information to estimate how much land would be covered with water by a major flood. Maps that show floodplain boundaries are created based on the findings.

Each floodplain is divided into two parts. The *floodway* lies in the center. It includes the stream channel and the overflow areas that would have the fastest flow of water. The *flood fringe* lies on either side of the floodway. These are the parts of the floodplain likely to be covered with slow-moving or standing water during a flood. It's important to understand where the floodway and the flood fringe lie, and how the water that runs through them behaves. History has shown that this knowledge could save lives and property.

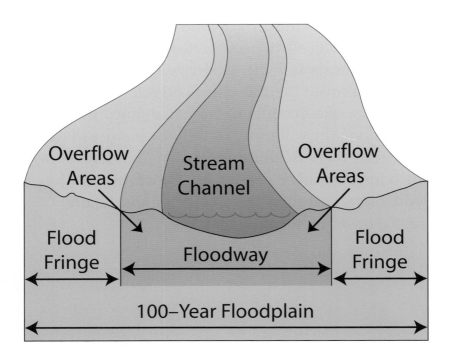

"A Roar Like Thunder"

One of the worst floods in the history of the United States took place on the floodplain in southwestern Pennsylvania's Conemaugh Valley. The valley was crisscrossed by several waterways. To the east, the South Fork of the Little Conemaugh River merged with several mountain streams to form the main waterway to Johnstown. To the west was the city of Johnstown, home to 30,000 people.

During the early nineteenth century, a dam was constructed near the South Fork, creating a large lake. This property had several owners before the South Fork Hunting and Fishing Club acquired it in 1879. The South Fork Dam was a simple 72-foot (21.9 m) high earth wall. It was quite different from the larger, more intricate dams built today. There were no built-in sensors to indicate possible weaknesses. If there had been, they would have shown that in 1889, the dam was in poor condition. It sagged in the middle. Discharge pipes needed to be replaced. Spillways were often clogged during heavy rains. Over the years, the owners of the dam had done little to maintain it. By 1889, the South Fork Dam could barely hold the millions of gallons of water behind it.

On May 30, 1889, the Conemaugh Valley area experienced heavy rain. An engineer who worked for the hunting and fishing club observed the water level of the lake rising an inch every ten minutes. The engineer knew that if the water topped the dam, it would break. A crew worked frantically to dig a new spillway, hoping to drain some of the water out of the lake. Workers piled dirt on top of the dam in an attempt to replenish the earth that was being eaten away by the water. Their efforts were too little, too late.

At about 3:00 P.M., the dam broke. Millions of gallons of water poured out of the lake, destroying everything in its path. A huge wall of mud and debris swept into the valley, following the Little Conemaugh River toward Johnstown. Along the way, it flattened the communities of Mineral Point and Woodvale.

The wall picked up speed as it roared down the valley. Telegraph lines stretched and snapped like elastic rubber bands. Trains were thrown from their tracks. Houses were ripped from their foundations. Trees snapped like toothpicks. People vanished beneath the churning rubble.

The entire mess became jammed up at a stone arch bridge that spanned the river. Nearly forty-five acres (18.2 hectares) were covered with oily, dirty debris. As night fell, the oily piles caught fire. Rescuers scrambled to free people from the blaze, but many who had survived the flood's first wave lost their lives in the flames. Property damage came to $17 million. It would take the people of Johnstown five years to rebuild their city.

Lessons Learned

After the Johnstown Flood of 1889, the citizens of that city realized they had to find ways to protect themselves. One local business, the Cambria Iron Company, proposed an interesting idea. Why not set up an escape route? They used old railroad parts to construct a vertical railway called an *inclined plane*. The inclined plane opened for business in 1891. It had two cars built to carry citizens safely to the top of a hill overlooking the city in case of another flood.

The railway saved many lives on March 17, 1936, when melting snow and steady rain caused yet another serious flood. Water rose to a height of fourteen feet (4.3 m) in some places. That night, half of Johnstown's citizens used the inclined plane to escape to the hills.

The 1936 snowmelt inspired the city of Johnstown to take serious steps to curb its flooding problem. Over the next five years, the city spent $8 million on a flood control program. River channels were widened and deepened. Strong, rigid flood walls were built along the banks of the Stony Creek and Little Conemaugh rivers to keep them from over-flowing. These improvements helped keep the city flood-free for many years.

The Government Steps In

It might seem that the problems faced by Johnstown and other old floodplain communities would discourage people from living on floodplains. In fact, that did not happen. As the population of the United States grew, old floodplain towns expanded. New communities sprang up on America's flood-plains. People felt the benefits outweighed the risks. The rivers provided easy transportation for goods and materials. Farmers could draw on them to irrigate crops. Residents liked living in homes with views of the water.

As a result, more and more flood damage was occurring each year. Finally, the federal government stepped in. In 1968, it set up a program that would help flood victims. To get that help, however, communities had to do their part to prevent future flood damage. There could be no new construction in the floodway portion of a floodplain. River crossings had to be designed a certain way. There could be no more low stone bridges like the one in Johnstown. Nothing could block the free flow of water away from populated areas.

New structures in the flood fringe areas had to be built. Foundations, or bases, of structures had to elevate them above 100-year flood levels. That way, water could not enter the buildings. Dams and flood walls had to be inspected regularly. If inspectors found a problem, it had to be repaired immediately.

Creating a Flood-Proof Environment

Communities were also encouraged to learn what to do to help prevent flooding. Trees and shrubs hold soil in place. Clearing away streamside forests can cause stream banks to collapse. Without this plant growth, rain flows more quickly off the land and into waterways. This fast-flowing water, called *runoff*, erodes the land. Floodplain communities had to preserve marshes and wetlands. Towns needed to restore native trees and plants along riverbanks in order to make the shoreline more stable.

Runoff is also a problem where there are paved areas. Unlike soil, pavement does not absorb rain. Streets and sidewalks can become elongated channels for fast-flowing floodwaters during bad storms. Adding storm drain systems helps to draw some of that water away. Setting aside land for parks and other green space can also give the rain places to drain.

Developing a Course of Action

While it is very important to know what to do to prevent floods, it is also important to know when they are likely to happen. Community leaders must monitor weather conditions during the flood season. Sustained periods of rain present as much danger as sudden, strong storms. Communication between weather centers and officials is critical.

Communication between community leaders and citizens is important as well. People need to know what to do and where to go in case of severe flooding. Alarm systems must be set in place. Cities and towns must set up evacuation routes and shelters where people can take refuge.

No Fail-safe Method?

The government's recommendations have helped many floodplain communities avoid the loss of life and property seen at Johnstown in 1889. There is no sure way, however, to stop floods from ever occurring. Even with all of Johnstown's preparations, that city suffered yet another flood in 1977, when over eleven inches (27.9 cm) of rain fell in just ten hours. Unless people can develop ways to control the weather, the threat of rising waters will continue to be a part of the underlying life on America's floodplains.

Did you know?

- Floodplains exist in all fifty states.

- A flood watch means that a flood is possible.

- A flood warning means that flooding is already occurring.

- A sudden flash flood can send a wall of water up to 20 feet (6.1 m) high.

- A car can be carried away by two feet of water.

- Just one inch (2.5 cm) of standing water can cause thousands of dollars in damage.

Think Critically

1. What is the difference between the two parts of a floodplain?

2. Explain the events that caused the Johnstown Flood of 1889.

3. Why was Johnstown's inclined plane created? What effect did it have?

4. Why did the federal government become involved in flood prevention?

5. Do you think it will ever be possible to prevent floods? Explain your answer.

 **Science**

Saltwater and Freshwater Make a list of bodies of water. Which ones are freshwater? Which ones are saltwater? List your findings in a two-column chart.

School-Home Connection Share the story of the dangers faced by the people of Johnstown in 1889 with family members. Talk about any dangerous situations that they may have been in that involved water.

Word Count: 1,591